AGING PARENTS & DILEMMAS OF THEIR CHILDREN

Aging Parents

&

Dilemmas
of Their
Children

by BERT KRUGER SMITH
JACQUELINE LELONG
BETTINA ADELBERG

PREFACE

A rectangle of light marked the ceiling of the bedroom when Mary A. opened her eyes. The air smelled delicately of lilacs, and she lay quietly by Jim, who was sleeping. Reality filtered through slowly.

Then, as if the air had turned suddenly heavy with rain, Mary felt the oppression of the day ahead. Mother's call late last night, the whining, accusatory tone of self-pity and anger. Then there was the doctor's appointment to which she had to take Mother— and the grocery shopping for her. Would the housekeeper come today after Mother had fought with her yesterday? Mary began to figure times. If she took a sandwich to the office, she could use her lunch hour for doing the doctor bit for Mother. And, if the housekeeper was there, Mary could leave Mother off and pick up the groceries and medications on her way home from the office.

If, if, if—the body which had been relaxed was now tense, and Mary could feel the beginning of a stomach ache. She jumped up so suddenly that Jim opened his eyes. Mary did not acknowledge his wakefulness. She hurried to the kitchen to put on the coffee, figuring times and possibilities as she did so. All of her life seemed to be filled with "managing." How to do a job, how to be a caring daughter, how to run a household, how to keep up with grown children. Even how to be a devoted wife. And finally, finally, Mary thought, feeling the nearby tears, how to have a minute to herself and peace to be a person.

3

Mildred and her mother had maintained an unusual relationship throughout her lifetime. "Just like two sisters," people used to say, seeing them together at lunch or at the movies. Mildred had her mother's soft blonde hair and deep blue eyes. They also shared a love of literature and occasionally attended the same classes.

Their relationship remained close even when Mildred's marriage took her halfway across the country. Letters and telephone calls plus occasional visits replaced the daily visits.

And thus the years passed. Mildred's two children grew up and away. One early morning as he slept, her gentle husband died as quietly as he had lived.

Mildred moved back to her early home to be close to her mother, now widowed. It would be return and renewal, she thought. But she had not reckoned with the years, which had struck her mother as a tornado would hit a tree, stripping her of the green leaves of her competencies and leaving the near-uprooted trunk bare and vulnerable to wind.

The irrational accusations, nocturnal telephone calls, wandering, and memory loss drove Mildred into her room in panic and in tears. The mother she had known had disappeared, and this mumbling, forgetful, incontinent stranger had replaced her. Where was selfhood, Mildred wondered? Was there a core of her mother within this other person?

Even more, what could she do, living as she did in close quarters? Would the remainder of her life be devoted to trying to keep her mother safe from harm, dry and clean? Mildred grew terrified that she was seeing herself a quarter century hence.

When Florence and Al brought Al's father to their house to stay, they did so with full discussion of what kinds of situations might surface with an addition to the family. After all, Florence and Al had always had a close relationship with their children and their parents, and they were sure the kids would accept Grandpa's presence with their usual adaptation. Shirley would be in college next year anyhow, and Mike was always off "doing his thing" with his high school cronies.

Thus, they moved Grandpa into the converted den, where he had his own television set and his own bathroom. Everyone seemed content—for the first six months. Grandpa spent a lot of time watching television; and when spring came, he asked for a section of the yard to plant a garden. Florence and Al congratulated themselves on their planning.

But then the loneliness caught up with Grandpa. The television wasn't enough, and he started following Florence around everywhere in the house, asking to join her on any errand. When Mike had company in his room, Grandpa wandered in and sat down. When Al was reading the evening paper, Grandpa wanted to talk. Shirley asked for a private telephone because Grandpa listened in on her calls, and Florence wondered if she could get a decent job anywhere.

When Grandpa slipped in the garden after a rain and suffered a broken arm, Florence locked herself in her room and wept, more for herself than for him. The whole family began to bicker in a way that they had not done previously.

"Honor Thy Father and Thy Mother," the Ten Commandments preached. Alice heard the words drumming in her head throughout her waking hours. Honor. What did that mean? Now that she had put Mother in the nursing home out at the edge of town, the remorse and guilt never left her.

As she typed reports, as she prepared a meal, as she shopped, Alice felt the guilt racing through her body like an underwater stream beneath a hill. Her mother in a nursing home. Why, Mom had cared for her through that long seige of mononucleosis when she was in college, had foregone a trip with Dad to New York when Alice had caught the mumps as a child, had come to be with her when her baby was born. And now—and now—she had shunted Mom off to a nursing home.

Alice's self-flagellation did not permit her to remember that Mother had set two fires in her kitchen because she forgot she was cooking food; that she had been in a near-coma one weekday because she had taken the wrong medicine; that she sometimes wore three dresses at once or put on none at all. That it was no longer possible for Mom to live in her own home and to be safe in any way.

Nor could Alice's family comfort her. They were willing to try, even though they were unwilling to go to the nursing home except under duress to visit the old woman who no longer recognized them nor seemed glad to see them. There was only Alice—and her guilt—and her mother in the nursing home.

Mary A., Mildred, Florence and Al, and Alice do not know one another. They do not live in the same town nor under the same circumstances. Yet they belong to one of the fast-growing groups in today's society—adult and aging children whose very old parents are needful of special care and attention.

The problem of "what to do with Mother (or Dad)" becomes an all absorbing one for multitudes of people. In a society where more than 50% of the women work, where nuclear families are removed from close and caring "others," where the over-75 age group is growing faster than any other segment of our population, the dilemma of how to cope when parents grow increasingly needful is one which many people are trying to solve.

The statement that "our parents took care of their own and also looked after us; yet we are unwilling to tend to them as they have special needs" is made frequently. Although it holds some truths, it is not the entire truth of itself. The situation of an enormous population of old people has not existed before in this country, where in the early 20th century only one person in 25 was 65 or older. That number jumped to one in ten by 1970, to one in 8 or 9 by 1980, and it is predicted that it will be 1 in 5 by the early 21st century.

Longer years have brought with them increasing fragility and, for some, increasing mental disability. Many of the frail elderly have needs so complex that any household would be taxed to care for those persons without professional assistance.

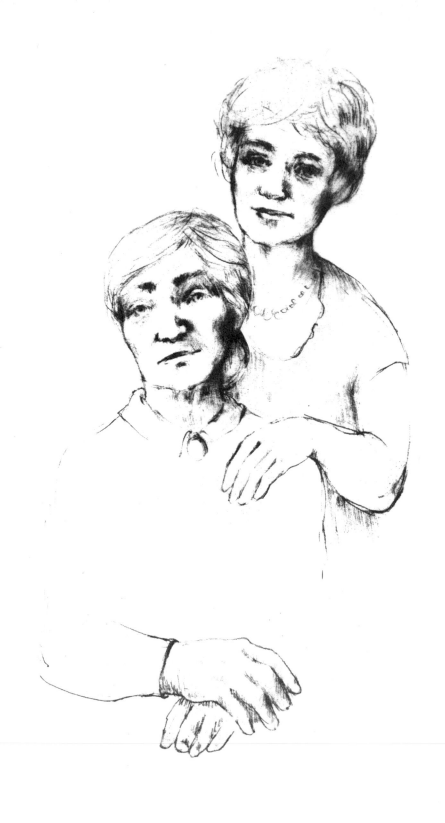

AGING PARENTS
AND DILEMMAS OF THEIR CHILDREN

What does it mean to grow old in our society? For some it means adding other beads on the abacus of existence. They are the ones who have maintained vigor, have stayed in good health, and have developed interests which keep them involved and alert. They are the ones who do not fall into pools of self-pity nor rail against fate because the years have passed. They maintain close friendships and loving relationships; they stay in the heart of life.

For others, growing old means loss. Loss of looks, of health, of job, friends, pleasures. Too often it means loss of ability to function in a fast-moving society. It often spells withdrawal, isolation, and loneliness.

In a society which has long worshipped youth, being old is negative. The laws about mandatory retirement at age 65 have meant that many men, most particularly, have been "set aside" before they were ready to lay down their work competencies. The great push for youth has made many women and men feel that wrinkles signify decay and that "older" is not better but far worse than being young.

When old people comprised only a small percentage of the population, their presence did not make for "problems." Most families were rural and settled. Thus, a caring community of family and friends was generally close at hand. In the non-rush atmosphere of daily life, those people who were old could find tasks to do and useful chores to accomplish.

Aging was simply a fact of life for a small percentage of people.

But the Industrial Revolution and the development of urban growth of the 20th century altered many lifestyles. Families became increasingly mobile; husbands were transferred to other parts of the United States; people began to live longer —and were caught up in a hurried, modular style of living which did not always make allowances for the old or disabled.

America, young America, bragged on its youth. It was a new society, vigorous and energetic. Old houses were torn down; new ones became the vogue. Longtime customs were replaced; fresh patterns were instituted. The media picked up the theme. Ads and commercials selling cars, shampoos, perfumes, or skin creams used models who were young, lovely, and supple. The elderly were pictured as having slipping dentures or irregularity.

In line with the self-fulfilling prophecy, then, people growing older, unless they had a strong sense of self, also began to feel that they were growing "lesser." Preparation for aging had not been part of the life experiences of most people in the early and mid-twentieth century. In fact, growing older was a personal affair, and most people met the experience in a way that they could manage best.

Legislation concerning Social Security, which began in 1936, and the Administration on Aging amendments which signaled the expansion of the nursing home industry raised concerns about institutionalization of the aged.

For many of the poor elderly such programs spelled salvation in terms of some financial and living aid. The increasing numbers of old people brought still more programs, such as the nutrition sites which sprang from Title VII of the Older Americans Act and the transportation efforts growing out of further amendments to the Act in 1975.

The protective devices which were aimed at giving security to a large population of older people took care of many physical needs. What still remained were the societal attitudes that new was good and old was bad. The roles which many people had held throughout their lifetimes—roles of spouse, worker, parent, volunteer, companion, and others—began to drop away, and society was faced with the problem of numerous old people locked into the prison of their loneliness. Recognition came that social and psychological needs of those persons were as great as the physical ones, and innovation began in terms of social programs.

10

FOR THE "CHILDREN"

If older people often suffered from lessening of options and withdrawal from society, their offspring also were often caught in a "no win" situation. Frequently the women—the customary caregivers—were hammered thin emotionally between the needs of children growing up and parents growing frail. They often found themselves with depleted inner resources for meeting the needs of both generations.

Or, because the population of the frail elderly is increasing at twice the number of the "young old" and at twice the rate of the total population, the most recent phenomenon is that of couples facing their own retirement and suddenly being responsible for old-old parents whose needs are great. Couples who have planned carefully for their retirement days, who wanted to travel or to study or to indulge in many hobbies, are unexpectedly homebound by care of a needy parent. Or, if the parent is in a nursing home, the "children" still bear the responsibility for frequent visiting and care.

What does it mean to have parents growing old and frail? To different people, different things. For some it means new responsibility at a time when their own needs are increasing. For others, it means fear that they are looking into the mirror of their own aging and mortality. For still others it may mean overriding guilt—guilt that they have neglected the parents in the past, unrealistic guilt that they have permitted the parents to grow old; love for the parents who once comprised the world for a youngster; sadness that the powerful have become so powerless; and often, hostility against the parent who has dared to become so needy and to demand so much.

Sorting out the options may be an overwhelming task when one is emotionally bound in the problem. Many feelings are intertwined like jungle vines around a tree. When a situation is unchangeable, attitudes about it must be altered. Such is the case with the families of parents who are old and frail.

11

The psychological punishment which the "children" give themselves can be nothing but unproductive for themselves and for the parents, who are at some periods aware of the difficulties their infirmities are imposing.

It sounds overly simplistic: Parents took care of young, helpless and dependent infants and children; those children, now grown, should take care of the frail and dependent parents. However, bringing up a child and caring for a frail elder are not analogous. While parenting is demanding, it brings delights as children develop and grow normally, as they build competence and skills. By comparison, the physical and emotional demands of a handicapped child drain a parent. The latter more closely parallels the situation of the adult son or daughter with an aging parent who is dependent and incapable of self-care.

The frail parent, especially one suffering from organic brain syndrome, often makes demands requiring full attention of one person. The adult "child," experiencing needs of several generations, may suffer exhaustion, guilt, and uncertainty. Parents of a child whose needs are enormous and unending may go through many of the same conflicts as adult children in trying to decide whether home or institutional care is preferable for a loved one.

"CHILDREN" LEARN THROUGH DISCUSSION

Caught between the care and guidance of the young, the increasing vulnerability and dependency of the old, and the responsibility of earning a livelihood for the nuclear family, middle-aged children experience inordinate stress amplified by guilt. It is the guilt that causes them to deny themselves the help needed in caring for or coping with elders. It is the guilt that breeds an overwhelming sense of failure when they cannot handle family problems privately or gracefully.

Sometimes the demands threaten the security of the family situation and shake one's sense of competence as a daughter or son. Yet people expect somehow to rise above these challenges in order to solve family problems alone. For example:

A woman in her 40s, accompanied by a child of ten, finds her way to an agency office. She is obviously nervous, and as she speaks she begins to cry. She has been caring for her invalid mother for fifteen months, having quit her job to do so. She is worried because the bedsores on her mother's back are not responding to the treatment prescribed by their physician. She is upset because the doctor will not visit the house to examine the old woman, and she finds it too difficult to transport her mother to the office.

The woman wants a name of a doctor specializing in geriatric medicine who will make housecalls. But as her story unfolds, it becomes obvious that she needs more than a doctor to visit her mother; she needs respite from the unending demands of caring for a bedridden person 24 hours a day. She needs someone to understand what she has endured and what she is facing. She finally says, "I hope they put her in the hospital. I need a vacation." Yet the tears indicate the shame she feels in seeking help, in admitting that she can no longer do it all by herself.

It is the "I can do this alone" syndrome which places family members' mental health at risk. The truth is that one sometimes is not able to do it alone, that people need one another to share information and understanding. They need one another to listen, to be accepting, and to offer emotional support during difficult times.

Out of this expressed need a service for families of the elderly was developed in 1974 by Child and Family Service, Inc., of Washtenaw County, Michigan. The agency offered a series of discussions designed for small groups. The objectives for the families were to learn about the aging process, to become informed about the available community resources, to explore possible strategies in response to individual problems, and to share personal feelings in the process. Alida Silverman, M.S.W., Coordinator of Older Adult Services, was

13

the moving force behind this innovative program which came to be known as "As Parents Grow Older" (APGO).

In 1978 the Administration on Aging, Department of Health, Education and Welfare, awarded a 30-month grant to the Institute of Gerontology, University of Michigan, to develop, implement, and evaluate the APGO model in collaboration with Child and Family Service of Michigan, Inc. Project leaders of "The Development and Evaluation of Educational and Support Groups for the Families of the Aged" produced a comprehensive manual of the model, trained facilitators in its use, monitored the progress of the family programs in ten sites, and designed an evaluative pre-and post-group questionnaire. The resultant assessment of the project underlined the fact that the APGO program was considered beneficial by the majority of families served.

The Hogg Foundation for Mental Health responded favorably to a request for funding for a similar pilot program in Texas which included an important variation. Because the Foundation is interested in programs which are innovative and which might be replicated elsewhere, this particular project had special appeal. It was aimed at providing support and information for families. It was also directed toward helping professional caregivers develop special understanding on behalf of the people they serve.

The mental health aspects were apparent immediately. If discussion groups could help to unlock some of the negative feelings and could aid persons in expressing emotions and sorting out reality from emotional hangover, then the younger family members could function more effectively and the older relatives would benefit.

One important modification was included in the second project. The concept of education and support groups for families of the aged was expanded to include a design to serve a special group of adult children—those facing the trauma of nursing home placement of an elder. The Texas Association of Homes for the Aging, the membership organization of nonprofit retirement and nursing homes, served

14

as the sponsoring agency for this Hogg-funded program.

The mission was twofold. First, educational support groups were conducted for two separate groups of families—those who were trying to keep their elders functioning in the community and those for whom nursing home placement was a reality. Second, workshops describing the APGO model were held throughout Texas, acquainting nursing home administrators and staff with the concepts and procedures of this family education program. The manual produced for this training phase was adapted from the University of Michigan training manual.*

The Texas Association of Homes for the Aging (TAHA) has continued to sponsor the APGO program in Texas. As a result of a proposal written by the Director of Special Projects for TAHA, the Texas Department of Human Resources awarded a grant to TAHA to disseminate "As Parents Grow Older" in four communities: Abilene, Edinburg, Dallas, and Fort Worth. Four teams of co-facilitators were recruited and trained, then monitored and evaluated. In this case, only the community-based model was used, placing the focus on those families who were committed to helping their elders stay as vital and self-reliant as possible in their own homes.

The primary objective was to provide information on the aging process and on community resources available to the family. This objective dovetailed with the statewide thrust of the Texas Department of Human Resources toward community care for those elders who were previously candidates for nursing homes at the Intermediate Care II level (in essence, personal care with administration of medication).

With the funding from the State of Texas, the APGO program gained new ground. It became an ancillary service in support of the caregiving families of elders who assume the responsibility for the care of their frail, dependent elderly relatives.

*See page 23 for procedures to obtain this manual.

15

PROCESS AND PROGRESS

Through the small group experience, adults with aging parents or relatives gain practical knowledge that helps them understand their older relatives' changing needs as well as their own feelings and actions toward these needs. In addition, the group provides an opportunity for adult children to express openly their shared concerns, to recognize alternative strategies for dealing with those concerns, and to acquire the necessary skills to cope with the problems of their aging families as well as to learn of community resources available to them.

DESIGN AND CONTENT

The APGO groups range in size from about 10 to 16 members. In most groups more than one family member is present as husbands and wives attend together as well as some sibling pairs. Group sessions are led by two co-facilitators trained for this program. Groups meet for six two-hour sessions. Topics of the community-based APGO model provide a different focus for each meeting: (1) Increasing understanding of the psychological aspects of aging, (2) Chronic illnesses and behavioral changes with age, (3) Sensory deprivation and communication, (4) Decision making and alternative living situations, (5) Availability of community resources, and (6) Dealing with situations and feelings.

Similarly, topics of the nursing home APGO model sessions are as follows:
(1) It happens to the family, not to the parent alone: adjusting to life in a nursing home, (2) Increasing understanding of the psychological aspects of aging, (3) Chronic illness and biological changes with age, (4) Mental impairment; depression; reminiscence as a therapeutic tool, (5) Sensory deprivation and communication, and (6) Family and staff; roles and interaction.

16

Each session incorporates both the educational and peer support components of the program as a whole. Audiovisual aids and print materials are utilized. Participants make specific applications of the material to their family situation: "Have I really considered how important it is for my parents to stay in their own home?" "Am I overprotecting my father and treating him like a child?"

GROUP PARTICIPANTS AND PROBLEMS

The participants come with a diversity of problems. Some of them are already providing care for an elderly relative when they enroll in the APGO group, while others are anticipating taking on this role in the future. Some common areas of concern expressed by family members are:

Emotional and behavior changes. "Mother has become increasingly withdrawn and depressed since father died. Her social isolation has made her increasingly dependent upon me. I need some advice on what I might do."

Health. "My father has been getting very forgetful and disoriented lately. The doctor says he is just 'getting old,' but I would like to understand more about what may be happening."

Living arrangements. "My parents are living on their own in another state. My father has been caring for my mother whose health continues to deteriorate. I would like to have them move closer, but they insist that they are managing. At what point do I need to take action?"

Family interactions. "My husband retired just a few months before my mother's illness. I am constantly feeling torn between her needs and his, not to mention my own. I am looking for better ways to cope with this situation."

Need for community services. "My father had been living alone until eight months ago when he broke his hip. He has heart problems, also, and I just cannot leave him for any long period of time. I need to know what services are available so that I might be able to get away from time to time."

As families try to make decisions about and cope with dependent elderly relatives, they have few models to follow and few people to turn to for guidance. Circumstances have changed in the lifetime of the elders. More women are working and so are less able to care for their relatives themselves. More people are living longer and so are more likely to deteriorate physically, requiring greater amounts of care. Geographic distance between family members widens, making family caretaking, decision making, and support more difficult.

Members of the APGO groups realized these benefits:

1. *Discovery that other families face similar problems and experience similar emotional pressures.*
   Charles and Evelyn had become very concerned about the welfare of Charles' mother who lived alone but needed more and more help to do so. She was having trouble getting around, and she was forgetting to take her medication. Sometimes she forgot to eat. When Charles and Evelyn turned to friends for advice, their concerns were made light of. Their friends had not yet had to deal with similar problems, and discussion of the difficulties aroused threat rather than sympathy. Charles and Evelyn were relieved to find others who could relate to their concerns and even offer some suggestions.

2. *The opportunity to put things into perspective by observing others at different stages of similar problems.*
Dorothy, mother of four, had just put her parents into a nursing home. She was experiencing a great deal of guilt that was exacerbated by her mother's loud complaints about her father's unhappiness. She and her mother never got along very well. Dorothy relaxed somewhat upon hearing about the adjustment periods of others' parents to the nursing home as well as suggestions for how to make her visits less difficult, such as bringing someone else along.

3. *Logistical support through the sharing of strategies, tasks and objectives.*
Participants' stopping in to see someone else's parent in the nursing home in which the parents of both resided . . . one participant lending bath rails to another . . . group members sharing information about such topics as wheelchairs, apartments, physicians, beauticians who make house calls, "how I got my mother to . . ."—the kind of information that is difficult to get in any other way.

4. *Reduction in apprehension as they acquire accurate information about aging:*
"Senility" is a wastebasket term that obscures the reality of reversible or at least treatable symptoms . . . anger and depression are common reactions to the losses experienced in the aging family by both elderly parents and their adult children . . . some doctors are more attuned to the needs of older people than others . . . an elderly person's withdrawal from social interaction may be due to gradual age-related hearing loss.

5. *Emotional release through expressing feelings and frustrations and receiving concerned attention.*
Margaret could not easily let up on her responsibili-

ties toward her mother, although she was in her 60s herself. She savored the opportunity to vent some of her frustrations among understanding others. Wanda remarked in her group evaluation that she felt that others sincerely cared about how both she and her mother were doing.

Just as there are many advantages for group participants, there are some limitations to the effectiveness of group intervention. Groups are not cure-alls nor are they the exclusive means of changing behavior. Members do not leave with their family situations all in order. However, they have been exposed to new information and the opportunity to see how other families cope. What they choose to do about their family situations will depend upon consideration of a number of factors that will be different for each family.

Not all people are suited for groups. Some people are suspicious or hostile or too fragile to benefit from a group experience. The kind of help needed by some family members may very well be beyond the scope of the group, requiring instead the services of a professional psychotherapist. Appropriate referrals are made under such circumstances.

The success of the APGO group in serving the needs of participants depends to a large extent upon the ability of the facilitators to create an environment that is safe, supportive, and accepting enough that people feel free to share their feelings and concerns. Discussing private family matters as well as one's reactions to them is not easily done before strangers.

Facilitators are chosen not only for their expertise and personal styles but also for the degree to which they get along well together—the extent to which they are likely to respect and even enjoy one another. Group members are put at ease by obvious camaraderie and enjoyment between facilitators. Humor and lightness are as important to the family groups as warmth and acceptance. The self-disclosure of facilitators who also are or have been in the same situation as group members sets the tone at the outset for openness.

POSSIBILITIES FOR THE FUTURE

The frail elder, his special concerns and problems, and the dilemmas of his family are here to stay in our society. If predictions concerning turn-of-the-century demographic data are correct, over 15 percent of the population—30 million people—will be over 65 in 2000.* And the "old-old" proportion of that group is ever increasing.

The greying of society and the implications for public policy and for private philanthropic policy are inescapable. Whose responsibility is it to care for the weak, the vulnerable, the dependent—at both ends of the life cycle? Traditionally, it has been the family. It seems unlikely that will change. What is likely to change is the proportion of families affected by the rapidly expanding population of frail elderly. More and more families will feel the impact on their resources, on their time, on their energy and on their emotions.

At the same time that the pool of families needing support is growing, the services for the elder members of these families are threatened by lack of funding. The flow of federal dollars is diminishing. The trend in long-term care is away from intensive nursing care toward personal care and more community care. This is a welcome trend. Yet, what of gaps in service? What of the woman caring for her invalid mother because the parent's social security benefit is too high for her to qualify for Medicaid but it is also too low to meet private costs in a nursing home? The daughter, unable to pay the difference out of her own income, is providing the 24-hour care that nursing home residents receive, but she is doing it alone. When the physical crisis—the running bedsores—comes, she eventually seeks help. She does not expect others to take over her problem, to solve it for her. She wants infor-

*Ellen Langer and Judith Rodin. "Aging Labels: The Decline of Control and the Fall of Self-Esteem," *Journal of Social Issues*, Vol. 36, No. 2, 1980.

mation; she wants to buy a service and does not know where to find a physician who specializes in the treatment of the aging.

If responsibility of care for an elder falls ultimately on the family, where does the responsibility lie for dissemination of valuable information concerning this care? In this culture education has long been one mandate of the community at large. The results of both the pilot project at the Institute of Gerontology, University of Michigan, and the Hogg-funded program in Austin, Texas, demonstrate that families experiencing anxiety related to the care of an elder have gained understanding of the aging process and of the older relative's needs and feelings. Sixty percent of the participants in the Michigan study reported improvement in identifying community services—a critical objective of the program.

Since the need for education concerning aging is great and universal, and the APGO program is demonstrably successful in educating families, then the question remains—how to disseminate the model program in the most cost-efficient manner? One answer is to absorb this model into the file of programs offered by existing social service agencies.

What are the agencies which might readily benefit from such a training package? The obvious ones—such as family counseling agencies, home-health services, mental health associations—easily come to mind. Others less obvious have historically served aging families in crisis but have not developed the counseling role until of late—hospitals, clinics and nursing homes. Other institutions which have only recently considered themselves responsible for serving their families are the industries—major employers of a work force more and more inclusive of women. Some major companies, enlightened about what is happening to the family in our society, now realize the importance of preventive mental health services for employees and provide 24-hour counseling. Staff personnel of these agencies and institutions will be better able to reach the families already integrated in their service system.

Another answer to cost-effective considerations is the use of a major institution in society which has been traditionally family oriented—the church. Within congregations of all faiths there is a wealth of talented people, social workers, nurses, doctors, teachers who are committed to the lay ministry movement. There are also many retired persons within the church whose store of experiences and training could be used in facilitating the APGO program for church families.

Admittedly, both volunteers and social service workers should be trained alike and should be monitored and evaluated alike by the their sponsoring institutions. A training module which could be easily transported to agencies, hospitals, nursing homes, industries, and churches would be valuable. It should include audiovisual materials which supplement the manuals (both community-based and nursing home), allowing people to be trained in less time, and present complex information in a more understandable, vivid form. The focus for the training workshop faculty would be primarily the demonstration of group process and facilitating skills.

The Area Agency on Aging would be the ideal umbrella instrumentality for training facilitators to use this educational program for aging families. Practical ways to enhance the future care of our elders are needed, ways which do not drain the resources of society but which reinforce and support the natural network already in place—the elder's family.*

*The manual for the program "As Parents Grow Older" can be obtained for $12.50 from the Institute of Gerontology, The University of Michigan at Ann Arbor. Requests for information about the Texas program, "As Parents Grow Older in the Nursing Home," should be addressed to the Texas Association of Homes for the Aging, Box 14487, Austin, Texas 78761.

CONCLUSION

Mary, Mildred, Florence and Al, and Alice, participated in discussion groups in various parts of Texas. As they began to share their feelings, they started to recognize that they were part of a larger "family" of persons responsible for and concerned about parents with special and constant needs.

Al came reluctantly. Big Al. Silent Al. Without Florence's insistence, he wouldn't be in attendance at all. There wasn't anything wrong in the family, he argued. Dad was a little crotchety, and Florence was over-reacting. Besides, he grumbled, what would sitting around and talking family secrets do to help a situation?

Florence, however, persisted. It was she who had taken the initiative to learn about the discussion groups, and it was she who was determined that if the current situation could be improved, she would find out how.

It took three sessions and some skillful leadership before Al could talk before the group, before he could talk about his red-faced farmer father who taught him how to fish and hunt and live. Big Al suddenly seemed both vulnerable and dependent; and with the support of the group, who listened and responded, Al became aware of his over-protective actions toward his father. At the same time he empathized with his father's loneliness and needs, as well as Florence's legitimate claim for privacy.

With renewed recognition, they were able to work out some plans for Al's father. A nearby day activity center could provide relief for Florence and stimulus for Al's father. Both Al and Florence gained some insights about how to give some special attention to the older man and thus to diminish his need to seek such notice in negative fashion.

For Alice, the group discussion was catharsis. When she knew that all of the participants who had parents in nursing homes shared feelings of guilt mixed with anger, she became willing to talk about her own emotions. The group discussion did not change the situation under which she lived. Her mother was still in a nursing facility. Alice was still the person who had put her there. However, what did change was her attitude toward herself and toward her mother.

The group had shared her sense of sadness that her mother needed such care; they responded with empathy to her feeling of hopelessness and fatigue. On a practical basis, they also aided her to see that visiting the nursing home every day was self-punishment for her and that she could serve her mother more lovingly if she could space her visits and give herself more breathing room.

"They are all you think about. It consumes your whole life."

Mary and Mildred, too, were able to gain new coping skills through the group discussions. Mildred's fear that she would turn into her mother was one which many people shared, she discovered. Discussion about research breakthroughs in the area of senility gave personal hope. Mary learned that her daily load needed lightening by others around her. Practical means of "weightlifting" were examined, and Mary learned to see that rewards for martyrdom were limited.

"It's such a relief to know I'm not the only one who feels at a loss sometimes."

The "solutions" sound simple. However, as therapists know from working with troubled people, gaining insight is a complicated and sometimes painful process.

Everything learned in the groups could have been discovered personally. However, the combination of skilled leaders and involved participants helped to clarify situations and to speed understanding. The very act of sharing, sorting, and discovering feelings helped to give credence to problem solving. Persons who had felt themselves alone and helpless in situations soon discovered that they were part of a large group and that there were positive actions which could be taken.

Sharing problems is always helpful. Sharing under the leadership of people who can direct one in positive directions is therapeutic.

Mary, Mildred, Al and Florence, and Alice can all attest to that fact. They represent the dozens of other persons who have been part of such discussion groups. In a world growing older, such techniques may prove to be an important mode of primary intervention for many people.